Remember to Record the Following:

- The mileage of every trip you make.
- The purpose of each business trip e.g. visiting a customer.
- The destination (and starting point) of each trip.
- The odometer reading at the beginning and the end of every trip.
- The driver's name.

Please Note:

- Use one record book per vehicle.
- Private mileage includes return travel from home to usual place of work, and all personal trip including holidays.

Good2go Vehicle Mileage Book

Vehicle Registration No.

____

DATE	NAME	ROUND TRIP		ODOMETER	
		FROM	TO	START	FINISH

TOTAL MILES BUSINESS	REASON FOR TRIP	TOTAL MILES PRIVATE

DATE	NAME	ROUND TRIP		ODOMETER	
		FROM	TO	START	FINISH

TOTAL MILES BUSINESS	REASON FOR TRIP	TOTAL MILES PRIVATE

DATE	NAME	ROUND TRIP		ODOMETER	
		FROM	TO	START	FINISH

TOTAL MILES BUSINESS	REASON FOR TRIP	TOTAL MILES PRIVATE

DATE	NAME	ROUND TRIP		ODOMETER	
		FROM	TO	START	FINISH

TOTAL MILES BUSINESS	REASON FOR TRIP	TOTAL MILES PRIVATE

DATE	NAME	ROUND TRIP		ODOMETER	
		FROM	TO	START	FINISH

TOTAL MILES BUSINESS	REASON FOR TRIP	TOTAL MILES PRIVATE

DATE	NAME	ROUND TRIP		ODOMETER	
		FROM	TO	START	FINISH

TOTAL MILES BUSINESS	REASON FOR TRIP	TOTAL MILES PRIVATE

DATE	NAME	ROUND TRIP		ODOMETER	
		FROM	TO	START	FINISH

TOTAL MILES BUSINESS	REASON FOR TRIP	TOTAL MILES PRIVATE

DATE	NAME	ROUND TRIP		ODOMETER	
		FROM	TO	START	FINISH

TOTAL MILES BUSINESS	REASON FOR TRIP	TOTAL MILES PRIVATE

DATE	NAME	ROUND TRIP		ODOMETER	
		FROM	TO	START	FINISH

TOTAL MILES BUSINESS	REASON FOR TRIP	TOTAL MILES PRIVATE

DATE	NAME	ROUND TRIP		ODOMETER	
		FROM	TO	START	FINISH

TOTAL MILES BUSINESS	REASON FOR TRIP	TOTAL MILES PRIVATE

DATE	NAME	ROUND TRIP		ODOMETER	
		FROM	TO	START	FINISH

TOTAL MILES BUSINESS	REASON FOR TRIP	TOTAL MILES PRIVATE

DATE	NAME	ROUND TRIP		ODOMETER	
		FROM	TO	START	FINISH

TOTAL MILES BUSINESS	REASON FOR TRIP	TOTAL MILES PRIVATE

DATE	NAME	ROUND TRIP		ODOMETER	
		FROM	TO	START	FINISH

TOTAL MILES BUSINESS	REASON FOR TRIP	TOTAL MILES PRIVATE

DATE	NAME	ROUND TRIP		ODOMETER	
		FROM	TO	START	FINISH

TOTAL MILES BUSINESS	REASON FOR TRIP	TOTAL MILES PRIVATE

DATE	NAME	ROUND TRIP		ODOMETER	
		FROM	TO	START	FINISH

TOTAL MILES BUSINESS	REASON FOR TRIP	TOTAL MILES PRIVATE

DATE	NAME	ROUND TRIP		ODOMETER	
		FROM	TO	START	FINISH

TOTAL MILES BUSINESS	REASON FOR TRIP	TOTAL MILES PRIVATE

DATE	NAME	ROUND TRIP		ODOMETER	
		FROM	TO	START	FINISH

TOTAL MILES BUSINESS	REASON FOR TRIP	TOTAL MILES PRIVATE

DATE	NAME	ROUND TRIP		ODOMETER	
		FROM	TO	START	FINISH

TOTAL MILES BUSINESS	REASON FOR TRIP	TOTAL MILES PRIVATE

DATE	NAME	ROUND TRIP		ODOMETER	
		FROM	TO	START	FINISH

TOTAL MILES BUSINESS	REASON FOR TRIP	TOTAL MILES PRIVATE

DATE	NAME	ROUND TRIP		ODOMETER	
		FROM	TO	START	FINISH

TOTAL MILES BUSINESS	REASON FOR TRIP	TOTAL MILES PRIVATE

DATE	NAME	ROUND TRIP		ODOMETER	
		FROM	TO	START	FINISH

TOTAL MILES BUSINESS	REASON FOR TRIP	TOTAL MILES PRIVATE

DATE	NAME	ROUND TRIP		ODOMETER	
		FROM	TO	START	FINISH

TOTAL MILES BUSINESS	REASON FOR TRIP	TOTAL MILES PRIVATE

DATE	NAME	ROUND TRIP		ODOMETER	
		FROM	TO	START	FINISH

TOTAL MILES BUSINESS	REASON FOR TRIP	TOTAL MILES PRIVATE

DATE	NAME	ROUND TRIP		ODOMETER	
		FROM	TO	START	FINISH

TOTAL MILES BUSINESS	REASON FOR TRIP	TOTAL MILES PRIVATE

DATE	NAME	ROUND TRIP		ODOMETER	
		FROM	TO	START	FINISH

TOTAL MILES BUSINESS	REASON FOR TRIP	TOTAL MILES PRIVATE

DATE	NAME	ROUND TRIP		ODOMETER	
		FROM	TO	START	FINISH

TOTAL MILES BUSINESS	REASON FOR TRIP	TOTAL MILES PRIVATE

DATE	NAME	ROUND TRIP		ODOMETER	
		FROM	TO	START	FINISH

TOTAL MILES BUSINESS	REASON FOR TRIP	TOTAL MILES PRIVATE

DATE	NAME	ROUND TRIP		ODOMETER	
		FROM	TO	START	FINISH

TOTAL MILES BUSINESS	REASON FOR TRIP	TOTAL MILES PRIVATE

DATE	NAME	ROUND TRIP		ODOMETER	
		FROM	TO	START	FINISH

TOTAL MILES BUSINESS	REASON FOR TRIP	TOTAL MILES PRIVATE

DATE	NAME	ROUND TRIP		ODOMETER	
		FROM	TO	START	FINISH

TOTAL MILES BUSINESS	REASON FOR TRIP	TOTAL MILES PRIVATE

DATE	NAME	ROUND TRIP		ODOMETER	
		FROM	TO	START	FINISH

TOTAL MILES BUSINESS	REASON FOR TRIP	TOTAL MILES PRIVATE

DATE	NAME	ROUND TRIP		ODOMETER	
		FROM	TO	START	FINISH

TOTAL MILES BUSINESS	REASON FOR TRIP	TOTAL MILES PRIVATE